Queen Maud
Range

Beardmore
Glacier

O. Evans
died here

SOUTH
POLE

Captain Scott's
last journey
to the
South Pole

Series 561

The story of Captain Scott's journey to the South Pole tells of the courage, determination and devotion of five brave men who sacrificed their lives in a great adventure.

Published by Ladybird Books Ltd Loughborough Leicestershire UK
Ladybird Books Inc Lewiston Maine 04240 USA

Captain Scott

by L DU GARDE PEACH OBE MA PhD DLitt
with illustrations by JOHN KENNEY

Ladybird Books

CAPTAIN SCOTT

If you put a long knitting needle straight through an orange from top to bottom, the orange would spin round on the needle. The earth turns round in the same way, and the line through the middle, where the needle is in the orange, is called the axis.

The two ends of this line are the North Pole and the South Pole, and the areas round them are called the Arctic and the Antarctic.

These two regions are both cold and covered with ice and snow, but otherwise they are very different. Within forty degrees of the North Pole are Great Britain, half Europe, and the whole of Canada; within forty degrees of the South Pole there are only the frozen South Shetland Islands. At the North Pole there is no land: the South Pole is a great continent, as big as Australia and Western Europe put together.

The North Pole was reached in 1909, but no-one had succeeded in the more difficult march to the South Pole until 1911. Then two different parties set out at the same time, one led by a Norwegian named Amundsen, and the other from Cardiff led by an Englishman, Captain Scott, in a little ship called the "Terra Nova", an old Scottish whaler.

The "Terra Nova" was a small ship, but she was strongly built to resist the pressure of the ice. Because she was small she could not carry a great deal of coal for the engines, so she had sails to help her along when the wind was fair.

Because the expedition to the far off regions of the South Pole would be away for a long time, a great many stores of all kinds had to be carried. As there are no animals except seals, and nothing at all grows in the icy wastes of the Antarctic, all the food required by the officers and crew of the "Terra Nova" had to be stowed away on board from the beginning of the voyage.

To-day aeroplanes fly regularly to the great scientific base at the South Pole, but in 1911 men were only just beginning to fly and there was no aeroplane which could make such a long journey. So Captain Scott would have to travel on foot, with tents and food on sledges drawn by dogs and ponies.

These ponies came from Siberia and were used to snow and ice. Nineteen of them were embarked, slung in the air by large cranes.

6

In addition to the nineteen ponies there were thirty-four sledge dogs on board. The ponies and dogs were kept in stalls and kennels, but of course it was not possible to exercise them.

On the long voyage from New Zealand, where they were embarked, to the base to be set up on the Antarctic continent, all these animals had to be carefully looked after. They had also to be fed, which meant taking large quantities of hay and dog biscuits in the already overcrowded ship.

Captain Oates and Cecil Meares were in charge of the ponies and dogs. Meares had travelled all the way across Russia and Siberia to find the right sort of animals, and had brought them half-way round the world to New Zealand. On the journey he had come to understand them, and they had come to know and trust him.

This was very important because good sledge dogs are very fierce, many of them being much more like wolves than the tame dogs which we know. Coming from the cold climate of northern Russia they suffered from the heat on the way, and only recovered when the "Terra Nova" at last sailed into the Antarctic pack ice.

The "Terra Nova" sailed from New Zealand on November 25th, 1910. During the next six weeks she crossed the stormiest seas in the world.

A week after sailing the "Terra Nova" ran into the worst storm of the whole voyage. Not only was the ship overloaded, but much of the coal and oil, in large drums, was piled up on the deck. Here too were some of the ponies and dogs.

The waves were washing over everything, and soon ten tons of coal had to be thrown overboard to prevent it from smashing the cases piled under the bulwarks. At the same time the ship was rolling so badly that the dogs were only held by their chains from being washed overboard. Captain Oates never left the ponies, which were being continually washed off their feet by the great waves sweeping over the deck.

The ship was rapidly filling with water, and when the pumps became choked with loose coal, she was in great danger of sinking. Buckets were passed from hand to hand to bale out the water in the engine room, and when the storm blew out, the battered "Terra Nova" was lucky to be still afloat.

The first iceberg was sighted soon after the storm, and from then on the "Terra Nova" was sailing past great and small icebergs day after day. They looked like great lumps of sugar floating on the water.

Icebergs are found both in the Arctic and the Antarctic. They are the ends of glaciers, or rivers of ice, which come down from the high mountains, always being pushed onwards by the weight of snow and ice above them. These rivers of ice, often hundreds of feet thick, move very slowly, and always down hill.

When the mountains are near the coast, the glaciers in time reach the sea. The mass of moving ice is then pushed out over the water and great lumps break off. Some of these are very large indeed and weigh many thousands of tons.

Because ice is lighter than water, the icebergs float on the sea, but with only a small portion of each one above the water. Gradually the waves melt the ice, often into strange caves and shapes of gleaming whiteness. Many such icebergs were seen by the crew of the "Terra Nova". Some had holes right through them, worn by the wind and waves.

Before the "Terra Nova" reached the rocky shore of the continent of the Antarctic, a way had to be found or forced through many hundreds of miles of pack ice.

Pack ice floats on the surface of the water, just as do the icebergs, but until it becomes broken by storms, it is a flat sheet of ice, often extending for hundreds of miles. It is sometimes only a few feet thick, and then it is possible for a ship to break through it. At other times it is frozen to a depth of twenty or thirty feet.

When storms far away from the ice pack send great waves across the sea, the sheet of ice becomes cracked and broken. Pieces are pushed up by the waves, and pile up to a height of many feet.

But often the cracks widen as the pieces float away from one another, and ships can find their way through the pack ice by following these winding lanes. Then one of the sailors goes up into the crow's nest, high on the ship's mast, to look far out over the ice and signal to the helmsman which way to steer for the open water.

On Christmas Day, 1910, the men on board the "Terra Nova" were a long way from home. It was certainly a white Christmas, but when they looked out over the pack ice there were no friendly lights across the snow, and no church bells rang in the Christmas morn.

The "Terra Nova" was firmly frozen in. She had entered a crack in the pack ice, only to find that there was no way through. The lane by which she had come had closed up and frozen over behind her. The only thing to do was to wait for the ice to break up.

For the sixty-five men in the ship this meant that Christmas Day could be a holiday. They decorated their quarters with the gay flags they had brought for the sledges, and they had a Christmas dinner with plum pudding and mince pies, just as though they had been at home.

One of the officers in his diary says that they had a large box of chocolates to finish up with, and sang songs and Christmas carols until midnight. The penguins sat around outside the ship and listened to sounds that the Antarctic had never heard before.

Four days later the ice broke up and the "Terra Nova" sailed on, threading the lanes through the pack ice or crashing through with her iron stem where it was thin. At last Ross Island was reached.

Because of the ice it was not possible to sail the ship close up to the shore. More than a mile of rough pack ice separated the "Terra Nova" from the land, and many tons of stores had to be carried across it. First of all the ponies and dogs were brought ashore, so that they could run about again after their weeks of confinement on board ship. Then the three motor sledges were unloaded, but unfortunately one of them broke through the ice and was lost.

All day and through the light night of the Antarctic summer the unloading went on, whilst at the same time the carpenters were busy erecting the huts in which the shore party were to live during the winter.

In less than a week the whole of the stores had been landed and the scientific instruments carefully checked. Piles of baled hay and hundreds of boxes of food were strewn about on the desolate snow-covered beach.

Winter at home is summer in the Antarctic, and work could go on day and night because there the sun never sets. But soon the Antarctic winter would begin, and warm weather-proof huts had to be built, in which the men could live during the long dark months.

The huts had been made so that they could be put together quickly, and all the parts had been carefully numbered. They were what we call pre-fabricated, and all that was necessary was to fasten the right pieces together in the right order.

This sounds very simple, but there had to be enough room to house not only the men, but the ponies and all the stores. The dogs were hardy enough to live outside, even in a temperature of many degrees below zero.

The huts were built on a low spit of land with cliffs on both sides. Great glaciers filled the ravines, and behind, high snow-covered mountains stood out against the sky. To seaward the pack ice stretched to the horizon, broken by a few small rocky islands. There was no grass, and no trees could grow in such desolate country. The only living things were penguins and seals.

The South Pole was hundreds of miles from the base camp, and the journey to it would occupy many weeks. Captain Scott intended to take the ponies and dogs as far as possible, and this meant that a great deal of food would be needed for them, as well as for the men.

The sledges were too small to carry enough for more than a few days, so it was decided to make dumps of hay, biscuits, food and oil along the route to the Pole. These dumps were called depots.

By this time the Antarctic summer was nearly over. Soon day and night would both be dark. So Captain Scott and his men set out with ten sledges, drawn by ponies and dogs, with a ton of stores. The first depot was to be made as far south— that is towards the South Pole—as possible.

Travelling was very difficult, and at one point some of the men and ponies were carried out to sea on floating ice. On another journey a whole team of dogs fell down a steep crack in a glacier. They were all safely rescued, and depots were established ready for the summer journey.

During the Antarctic winter no journey could be made. The sun never rose above the horizon, and storms and blizzards of frozen snow were almost continuous. The cold was so intense that the men could not stay out of the hut for more than a few minutes.

Inside the hut it was warm and light, with good food and even a gramophone and a piano. There was also plenty of work to be done, and everyone was kept busy.

As well as making the journey to the South Pole, Captain Scott's expedition was gathering all sorts of scientific information about the weather and the ice and the conditions to be met with during the winter months in the Antarctic. The scientists were taking and recording their observations, and the men were occupied in preparing the equipment ready for the summer journey.

The main hut was divided into a number of small rooms around the sides, with the tables for meals down the centre. The scientists had their laboratories, the photographer his dark room, and so on. Captain Scott had a room to himself, and in it he was the busiest man of all, keeping records and planning the journey to the Pole.

The Antarctic winter passed, and with the sun again above the horizon for most of the day and night, Captain Scott determined to start on the long journey to the South Pole. Depots of food and fodder had been placed along the early stages of the route. Everything was ready.

Captain Scott's plan was to set off with as many men as possible, and all the ponies and dogs. Every sledge was heavily loaded, and at certain points on the march some of the men would dump their stores and return with just enough food to see them home. These stores were for Captain Scott's party on the return journey.

By October the weather was fine enough for a start to be made, and an advance party set out, hauling a number of fully loaded sledges with the two motors. This was to save the strength of the dogs and the ponies over the first rough ice.

Captain Scott followed with more men and the animals. Unfortunately the motors broke down owing to the intense cold and the rough going, so that soon the men, ponies and dogs were hauling all the sledges. It took them many hours to cover ten to fifteen miles a day.

It was six weeks since the advance party had set out and so far everything had gone well. But there was always the possibility of bad weather, and at the beginning of December they met with the worst blizzard they had yet encountered.

The driving snow, later turning to rain, covered everything. The ponies were given some shelter behind walls built of snow, but they suffered a great deal. The Siberian dogs simply curled themselves up in the snow and went to sleep.

In the tents everything was wet through, including the sleeping bags. But as there was nowhere else to go, and travelling was quite impossible, the men sat or lay in their wet sleeping bags for hour after hour, whilst melted snow dripped on them from above, and water rose higher above the floor of each tent. It was not only a miserable time for everybody, but they were eating up five days food without making any progress.

At last the blizzard ceased and the sun shone. Only the tips of the tents and the ski sticks, stuck upright in the snow, were to be seen. It was rightly christened "Shambles Camp".

The ponies had suffered greatly during the blizzard, and it was clear that they could not travel very much further. It would have been cruel to drive them forward in the deep snow, into which they sank at every step. The most merciful thing was to shoot them.

The sledges had now to be pulled either by the dogs, who were going well, or by the men. As the men were travelling on skis they did not sink into the soft snow as the ponies had done, and the dogs were used to such conditions. So for a time good speed was made.

During this time the party had been crossing the great ice barrier. This is really a frozen bay extending for hundreds of miles inland from the sea. Now for the first time they were on land, but it made very little difference, except that they began to climb up the great glacier which comes down from the high plateau of the South Pole.

In the meantime, unknown to Captain Scott, the Norwegian, Amundsen, was well on his way to the Pole by another and easier route. It was a race in which neither knew where the other one was.

The great river of ice, one hundred and twenty miles long, which now faced Captain Scott and his men, is called the Beardmore Glacier. This glacier had to be climbed before they could reach the high plateau of the South Pole.

All along the route the depots of food and fuel, from which the returning parties were to pick up what they needed, had now been established. It was time for the dog teams to turn back. They had hauled the supplies for these depots over more than four hundred miles of snow and ice. From here onwards the remaining sledges had to be pulled by the men themselves.

They were now about four hundred and fifty miles from the South Pole, and still loaded with supplies for five more depots, as well as all the food needed for themselves on the way.

As they watched the dog teams disappear in the distance they could not help thinking of the long, weary haul they themselves had in front of them, compared with the cosy hut to which the drivers of the dog teams were returning. These were Meares and a Russian boy named Dimitri. All the long way back to camp they gallantly lived on half rations, so as not to take too much from the depots.

All glaciers have great cracks in them, caused by the breaking of the thick ice over the ridges in the rock below. As the ice is sometimes hundreds of feet thick, these crevasses, as they are called, are very dangerous. Often they are drifted over with snow, which forms treacherous snow bridges completely hiding them from view.

The broken ice of a glacier is never a flat plain like the barrier ice. The pressure of millions of tons of ice sliding down from higher ground pushes the ice below into great pressure ridges. Many of these had to be climbed or avoided.

The weather had now turned sunny and even warm—warm, that is, for that part of the world. We should probably think it was very cold indeed. But it was warm enough partly to melt the snow bridges over the crevasses and to make them very dangerous.

Christmas Day was also the birthday of one of the men. His name was Lashly, and he celebrated the day by falling into one of the deep crevasses. Fortunately he was held by the harness with which he had been hauling one of the sledges, and his comrades were able to pull him out.

After a depot had been set up at the top of the Beardmore Glacier, another of the supporting parties turned back. There were now only two teams of men left, pulling two heavily laden sledges southwards toward the South Pole.

These two remaining parties continued for another hundred and sixty miles, a journey which took fourteen days. Then the last supporting party built a depot containing all the supplies they could spare, and turned to face the return journey of more than seven hundred and fifty miles.

Day after day this party descended the treacherous Beardmore Glacier. Thick mist caused them to lose direction, and they found themselves amongst crevasses wider and deeper than any they had yet met.

Then Lieut. Evans was taken ill. When he could walk no more, his two companions, Lashly and Crean, tied him on the sledge and pulled it another hundred miles. They were within thirty-five miles of the forward base where men and dogs would be waiting, when a blizzard made it impossible for the two weary men to drag the sledge any further. The little tent was put up, and Crean went on alone to get help. It took him eighteen hours to cover the thirty-five miles.

Lieut. Evans, Lashly, and Crean arrived safely back at the base camp. Somewhere, hundreds of miles away, Captain Scott, Captain Oates, Lieut. Bowers, Dr. Wilson, and Petty Officer Evans were still struggling over the frozen waste of snow and ice.

It was one hundred and forty-six miles to the South Pole from the point where the last supporting party turned back. Captain Scott and his companions covered the distance in two weeks.

Their sledge was heavily loaded with their sleeping bags, a tent large enough for five men, and enough food to last them to the Pole and back to the first depot on the return journey. The snow was soft, and the sledge sank into it instead of sliding easily over the surface. One of them wrote in his diary that the sledge dragged like lead.

As they neared the South Pole their excitement grew. Other men had tried to reach it, but none had ever succeeded. They were to be the first. Then suddenly they stopped. In the snow, leading southwards, were the tracks of dogs and men. They were the tracks of Amundsen and his expedition, and as Scott and his party followed them, they knew that the Norwegians had won the race to the Pole.

Captain Scott reached the South Pole on January 17th, 1912. In a small tent, flying the Norwegian flag, he found a letter from Captain Amundsen wishing him a safe return.

After two days at the Pole, resting and taking observations, the five men turned to face the long journey of nine hundred miles back to the base camp. For more than two months, day after day, they were to drag their sledge over some of the most difficult and dangerous ice fields in the world, over treacherous snow bridges covering deep crevasses, and through snow-drifts into which they sank up to their waists.

At first the going was easier. With the wind now behind them, they rigged a mast and a small sail on the sledge: Lieut. Bowers wrote in his diary that it fairly slithered along with a fresh breeze.

This does not mean that the sledge was going like a toboggan downhill. It took them all day to cover sixteen miles, but on the way they had picked up supplies from the first depot on the homeward journey. This was very important. Only by going from one depot to the next could they hope to get off the plateau alive.

The wind which at first had filled the little sail and helped them on their way became a blizzard. The blinding snow made it difficult for them to determine the right direction. Soon one of the men had to hold on to a rope behind the sledge to steady it as the wind increased. But they were making good progress, and for the first two weeks all went well.

By February 4th they were on the great glacier, with crevasses on all sides of them, and both Captain Scott and Evans had bad falls. Evans was seriously hurt with a blow on the head, and they were obliged to camp until he recovered. This meant that they were eating up their food supplies without making any progress towards the next depot.

When they went on again Evans was only able to travel slowly. The weather became worse, with continuous storms and snow blizzards. Still they struggled on, until they reached the foot of the Beardmore Glacier.

Petty Officer Evans had been the strongest man of the party, but the effects of his fall, and the hard travelling on top of it, had proved too much for even his strength. On February 17th, he died.

There were now only four men left to do the work which had tried five men almost to the limits of their strength. Still they struggled on, fighting their way northwards against terrible weather conditions. On some days they were only able to cover four miles, after toiling at the sledge ropes for eight or ten hours.

The depots were about sixty-five miles apart, and each contained enough food to carry them on to the next one, at the expected rate of travelling of ten or twelve miles a day. At the much slower rate of advance their food was always exhausted before the next depot was reached. This made them weaker and slowed them up still more.

Further misfortunes were in store for them. The temperature fell to more than forty degrees centigrade below zero, and the snow froze to a fine powder. It was like pulling the sledge over soft sand.

Now another and even more serious misfortune overtook them. In each of the depots there was a store of fuel, upon which they depended if they were not to freeze to death during the bitterly cold nights. But the tins had leaked, and they were now as short of fuel as of food.

The bitterly cold weather and the biting winds had caused all the party to become frost-bitten.

Captain Oates was very badly affected. His swollen feet made every step an agony, and he had to be helped by men who had almost as much as they could do to drag themselves forward through the snow. Progress became slower than ever. On March 17th they camped for the night, in a temperature forty-six degrees below zero. It was Captain Oates' birthday.

The future seemed hopeless. They were more than a hundred and fifty miles from the base camp, and thirty miles from the next food depot. Their only chance was to press on whilst they had a little food left. But with a very sick man who could scarcely stand or walk, they were taking hours to cover a mile.

That evening, whilst a blizzard was howling round the tent, Captain Oates walked out into the bitter Antarctic night, saying that he would not be long. He had no intention of returning. He went to his death, knowingly and willingly sacrificing his own life in the hope that without him, his comrades might have a better chance to live.

Three men were left to face a hundred and fifty agonising miles of frozen waste between them and safety. They were weak from lack of food, frost-bitten, and terribly weary. They knew that they could only hope to cover four or five miles in a day of heart-breaking toil.

But they also knew that food and fuel were waiting for them at the next depot, thirty miles away. With aching limbs they put on the sledge harness and pulled against the sluggish weight of the sledge, sunk deep in the soft snow.

For hour after hour they struggled on, knowing only that they must not stop. Their minds numb with fatigue, they camped and went on again for four days and nights. At the end of it they had covered only about twenty miles.

When they looked out on the fifth morning, the air was thick with driving, blinding snow. The blizzard had struck again. It was the last misfortune. Eleven miles to the north of them were food and fuel. If they could reach them they could rest in the warm tent, with good food to restore their strength. Each hour they looked out of the tent, but the blizzard was blowing more fiercely than ever. Travelling was impossible.

For four days the blizzard blew. They had food for two days and fuel for one last meal. The temperature was forty degrees below zero.

Outside, the storm howled about the little tent. Inside, the three men, without food or heat, lay for hour after hour in their sleeping bags, the cold striking into their very bones and numbing their minds. With fingers which could scarcely hold the pencil Captain Scott made the last entries in his diary. "Had we lived," he wrote, "I would have had a tale to tell of the hardihood, endurance, and courage of my companions which would have stirred the heart of every Englishman. These rough notes and our dead bodies must tell the tale."

The blizzard blew itself out, but the little tent remained closed and silent. The polar winter descended upon the Antarctic. The sun never rose above the horizon; incessant gales and driving snowstorms made any attempt at rescue from the base impossible.

So ended one of the most gallant ventures in the history of our race. Courage, determination, and the highest sense of duty were defeated by the worst weather of the most savage climate in the world. No men could have endured more: none ever set a nobler example of heroism and devotion.

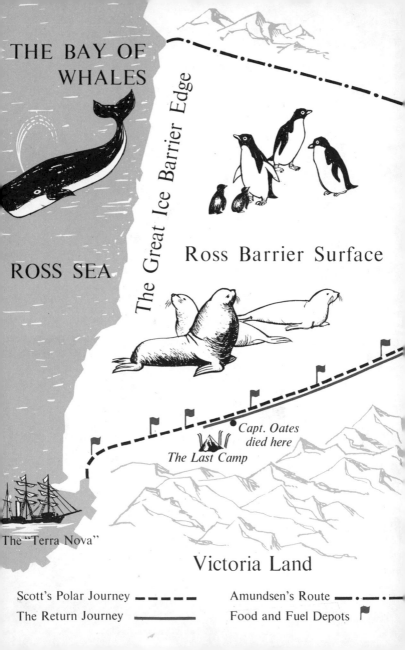

THE BAY OF WHALES

The Great Ice Barrier Edge

Ross Barrier Surface

ROSS SEA

Capt. Oates
died here

The Last Camp

The "Terra Nova"

Victoria Land

Scott's Polar Journey   - - - -   Amundsen's Route   - · - · -
The Return Journey   ————   Food and Fuel Depots   ⚑